Bilateral Asymmetry

Bilateral Asymmetry

by Don Riggs

Texture Press
Norman, Oklahoma

Texture Press
Managing Editor: Susan Smith Nash, Ph.D.
1108 Westbrooke Terrace
Norman, OK 73072
E-mail: texturepress@beyondutopia.com

Author photograph by Marjorie Becker
Cover by Arlene Ang
Book design by Valerie Fox

for W.M.
my ideal reader

Contents

Gallery Opening

Still Life / 15
Facets / 16
Experimental Innovation / 17
Fragonard Brushing / 18
Pagan Mystery in the Renaissance / 19

Dealing in Futures

Images / 23
Four of Pentacles / 24
Three of Swords / 25
The coin of the fifth / 26
Finger to Smile / 27

Stepping-Wolf Apollo

There Is an Arcane Pleasure in Flossing / 31
Supporting Role / 32
Cheirography / 33
Cancer Moon at Midheaven / 34
Myopic / 35
Regressed Memory / 36
Speculum Mundy / 37

Pet Scans

Occasional Cat / 41
1. The Educated Grasshopper / 42
2. Fall / 43
3. Sparrow / 44
4. Subway / 45
5. Ant, Alone / 46
Fourth House Thumbnail / 47
Crow / 48
The Flies of Mid-Autumn / 49

First Faceless

Fishing Story / 53
Background / 54
Agricultural Research Station, Beltsville, MD / 55
Can't Think / 56
Hugs / 57
Morning Mirror / 58
Nakedness / 59

Bilateral Asymmetry

Bilateral Asymmetry / 63
Fear and Symmetry / 64
Prescription / 65
The Elements / 66
Tickle Torture / 67

Cérémonie

Confession / 71
Sometimes I just sit / 72
Ossipoesis / 73
Private Intracies / 74
The Elves Know / 75
Cérémonie / 76

Ars Brevis Vitrina Obscura

Lying at the Base / 79
Priming the Pump / 80
Influencza / 81
Alignment / 82
Invisible Hand / 83
Reading Writing Rilke / 84
Uber Blumen und Madchen / 85
After Rilke / 86
Enjambment / 87
Inversion of, No Question / 88

Silent Echo

Pairing / 91
Convention / 92
Moon's Ode to Earth / 93
Long/Distance / 94

Hortus Conclusus / 95
Superhero Weakness / 96
Herself / 97

Grind of Being

Prize / 101
Boulot / 102
Reconfiguration / 103
Superfluity / 104
Real Magic / 105

Time Files

Now We Turn Two / 109
Soundings / 110
The last time we danced to the Beatles / 111
Reality Check / 112
When I die I hope they will play Mozart / 113
Winter Yin / 114

Acknowledgments

Some poems in this book previously appeared in the following publications: *Painted Bride Quarterly*, *Orizont Literar Contemporan*, *Press 1*, *Drexel Online Journal*, *Conscious Mapping: Poets Journey through Verbal Geography*, and *Poems for the Writing: Prompts for Poets*.

Heart-felt thanks to Paula Marantz Cohen, for her prescient assessment of my work in her fiction, Marilyn Piety and Brian Foley, for making up at least half my audience at many readings, Fred Siegel and Gail Rosen, for submitting themselves for my sake to evenings where people read from pieces of paper, Jacques Catudal, for recognizing the *daimon* in me, to Christopher Th. Nielson, for his Arnold Schwarzenegger imitation, to Lynn Levin for doing readings in tandem with me at the old Fringe Festival, to Kathy Volk Miller for publishing some of these poems; also to the 34th Street Poets Sandy Chaff, Barb Daniels, Betti Kahn and Cindy Savett, who workshopped many of the poems here (I still have your comments copied down on my typescripts of them) and Daisy Fried, Jim Quinn and Nathalie Anderson, who critiqued an earlier version of this book that never was published. Valerie Fox for her gentle but persistent nudging that led to my putting together these poems and drawings and her role as midwife, along with Arlene Ang, in the birthing of this book. To Daniel Dragomirescu, for bringing my poems to an international readership. Finally, to Petra, who explored the *cansos* with me and introduced me to the *Cantigas d'amigo*; she will find herself in here.

GALLERY OPENING

STILL LIFE

The poet at the desk, lit by a lamp,
surrounded by a dark study. Spines gleam
where the one incandescent bulb reaches,
the rest is in sharp-edged shadow. Elbows
rest on the flat wood, solid support
for shoulders stacked on top of infrastructure
of ribs, cathedral forever unlit
unless surgeons should be called upon

to probe the inner mechanisms the ghost
needs in working order to remain there.
Hands lie on the desk like an afterthought,
the page mostly blank, though there are scribblings
indecipherable to all, even
the one who wrote them, evidently, down.

FACETS

As Cézanne placed peaches on the table
and painted them, relentlessly captured
shadows—that is, light intercepted by
solids—he rearranged them on canvas,
and he moved them across the tablecloth
as if they were pawns in a game of chess.
He moved the cloth itself, bunching it here
and smoothing it almost flat over there.

Something about how the round of apples
broke into facets fascinated him,
and he recorded the way his mind cut
continuity into fragmented
digits, as if oranges were modeled
for fingers or intellects to grasp them.

EXPERIMENTAL INNOVATION
after David Galenson

The problem with emulating Cézanne
as someone who finds out where he's going
in his art simply by doing it, is
never knowing when you have arrived. Some
younger artist whose name you'd recognize
visited him and reported that he'd
take perfectly fine paintings and throw them
away in disgust or paint over them.

Furthermore, I'm tired of rearranging
fruit on tables, painting that damn mountain
for the thousandth time—facets and splotches!
I'd rather be like Renoir with those nude
models, brushing them voluptuously,
or Rodin, palpating clay into flesh.

FRAGONARD BRUSHING

It is because we lived so near downtown
Washington that in third grade we would go
to the National Gallery of Art
for an Introduction to Great Painting.

I brought back with me a reproduction
of Raphael's "St. George and the Dragon,"
but my sister Suze chose Fragonard's "Young
Girl Reading," which hung on her bedroom wall

for a decade. Every morning I gazed
at her pose, focused on the fictive acts
that take place not on the pages themselves,

but somewhere indefinable. Her soft
cheeks glow, and when I saw the real painting,
I saw that the brush strokes caressed her breast.

PAGAN MYSTERY IN THE RENAISSANCE

St. Jerome mistranslated the Hebrew
"rays" for "horns," so for a millennium
Catholics thought Moses with the Commandments
had sprouted horns—see Michelangelo's
sculpture of him, twisting Hellenistic
hero with well-defined musculature,
thoughtful fingers trailing through a stringy
beard, the progeny of Neptune and Pan.

Progeny, rather, of one of Neptune's
daughters, who sang amid the seaweed, sea-
wreathed, until the goat-god accompanied
her on his syrinx in the lassitude
of a summer afternoon and even
the stone man turned from his tablets to hear.

DEALING IN FUTURES

IMAGES

Images on cards dropped on the table
or placed, deliberately, on defined
spaces within the rest of the array;
images that surprise, that shock, like Death
grinning eyeless, mindless, that empty skull;
or a man hanged upside down by his feet,
the world reversed, blood rushing to his head.

Or images that please, promise pleasure,
like the naked lovers whose bodies twine
around each other in a warm handshake.

And sometimes images don't surprise
the Querent, whose question is pro forma,
because he knows nothing spectacular
is in his future, just lots of hard work.

FOUR OF PENTACLES

after a card by Boris Vallejo

She obviously wasn't born to wealth,
so the Pentacle tattooed to her glutes
emphasizes where she has set her sights.
Her senses are highly attuned to stealth
so even a slight breeze makes her alert
to the possibility of a theft,
though it be nothing more than a stray draft.
Constantly on guard, the fist of her heart
precludes the possibility of an
opening to another person in
her life. She is surrounded by treasure;
her muscles, highly toned, are all on edge
to defend her chests. No thought of pleasure
insinuates itself with a soft nudge.

THREE OF SWORDS

The heart may ask for pleasure,
     and open itself to a sword.
The heart may hope for treasure,
     and pain is its reward.
The heart may hope for lifelong love
     and get a searing sting:
the heart is punctured from above
     and then it has to sing.

The heart will cloak itself around
     with bleak and stormy weather
but when deflated, it will find
     its skin is tough as leather,
and Melancholy's gravity
     grown weightless as a feather.

THE COIN OF THE FIFTH

Everything I do is designed to make
sense: pay bills, correct grammar, mark papers,
and sure, I deal myself cards that tell me
to lean into the clay I shape and raise
on the wheel I spin with my foot treadle,
to stamp out identical many coins.
Yet the near future shows me morose, one
leg cut off at the knee, only the coins

of matter, emotion, intellect, and
nerve spread before me, the coin of the fifth
essence an undiscovered star that gleams
in the sky unseen by my lowered eyes.

Advice is to place myself on the pyre
and blast my body, fly with wings of flame.

FINGER TO SMILE

I am a flaming ship that arrives at last in a darkening harbor.
I am a man hanged upside down by his ankle.
I have been the Emperor, the Magician, competent, powerful, clever.
I am the Fool, blindfolded, a rabbit nibbling near my ankle.

I am a flaming staff reflected in the oil bead eye of the Salamander.
I am an old dragon, its slit eye hypnotic.
I am a fair wind, sharp as six swords, with nothing but a sail to inhibit it.
I am death, a skeleton amused by a joke unspoken.

I have been the Lovers, entangled in the meadow.
I'm the High Priestess, finger to smile, silent.
I have been the Fool, oblivious to the chasm.

I have been the Tower, the man thrown from its top with stones dislodged
      from under me.
I have been the Hierophant, replete with the panoply of esoterica.
I have been death and will be often before my body stops beating.

STEPPING-WOLF APOLLO

THERE IS AN ARCANE PLEASURE IN FLOSSING

There is an arcane pleasure in flossing
akin to the supreme joy of weeding—
grasping that fledgling tender leafy weed
by the narrow, flexible stalk between
forefinger and thumb and gently tugging
—gingerly, lovingly, almost hugging
the plant to encourage it to relax,
like sending energy through a massage

so the recipient will start to space
out, the small weedling will soften its roots'
grasp on the earth, one by one those fingers
will drift skyward, hypnotized, not break off
and remain buried, to regenerate
the uninvited plant another day.

SUPPORTING ROLE

I always identified with the sidekick
in buddy movies and TV spy shows—
Andy Devine sitting next to John Wayne
on top of the stage coach, or on The Man
from U.N.C.L.E., Illya Kuryakin, not
Napoleon Solo. Actually,
I really thought that Mr. Waverly
sitting behind his desk deep underground,

the brains of the operation, sending
his agents out into danger to put
his policies into action, was cool.
He was professorial, with his globes
and his maps and his herringbone jackets,
clearing his throat as he cleaned out his pipe.

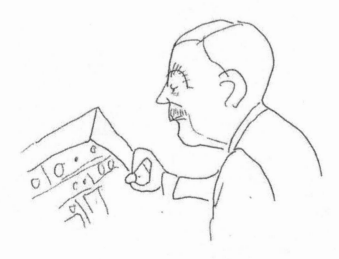

CHEIROGRAPHY

The arrondissement of my palm must be
the Fifth, for look—here is the Rue Descartes,
that rationalistic upbringing Dad
gave me as a child, and all the conflicts
between that and the Mount of Venus it
skirted, but the life line angles off—yes!

it is the Rue Mouffetard that steadily
descends between medieval rowhouses
in which I rented many a garret
above experimental theaters
and esoteric bookstores.
                     Finally,
at the base of the hill, the road fragments
and I take the Rue Pascal, terrified
of the silence of infinite spaces.

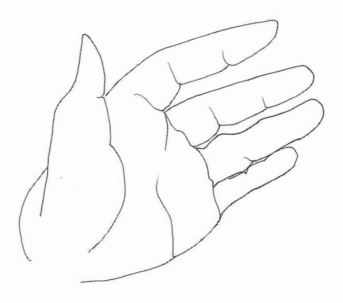

CANCER MOON AT MIDHEAVEN
Harry takes a night walk

Wherever I've lived, taken walks around,
I've had two souls, as Goethe has put it,
behind a single sternum. Some have found
the one soul outspoken, when I've let it

rip, making my extraversion a wall
behind which I hid. Instead of hard abs,
I'd hold my arms wide, as to embrace all;
few recognized them as the pincers crabs

raise in the air when stranded on a pier
dropped by a clumsy crabber from a net
finding that the carapaced one is set
on distancing itself from the open air.

I'd crawl back into my small apartment
to show the world I knew what *apart*
meant.

MYOPIC

to rhyme with "biopic"

I found my glasses in a dream last night
but couldn't recall where they were today.
I'll have to keep on wearing my old pair
and see the world the way I used to.
The difference isn't really that striking:
there's just a little bit more of a frame
to see things through, excluding some others;
peripheral vision is still quite vague.

I found my glasses in a dream last night.
My therapist asks me what that might mean.
"Wish fulfillment?" I ask. She stays silent,
watching intently as emotions play
across my face like the U.S. Open.
My naked eye reads my palm perfectly.

REGRESSED MEMORY

Before I'd developed as much control
as I have since, both as art and technique,
when I was a kid I peed in the pool,
although in that I was hardly unique.

No one could smell the odor of urine
as I felt my crotch grow suddenly warm
because of the high level of chlorine
in that acre of water. No real harm

was done, I'd tell myself, everybody
did it. Even now that I am aware
how shame culture differs from guilt culture,

I assure myself that my private thought
should make no difference to anybody,
but still hold it in, in case I get caught.

SPECULUM MUNDY

I hold my body back within my skin;
my clothing also holds my flesh within.
My feelings slosh around with all my blood
and inundate my brain with every mood.
I wonder: should I break now with my past?
I have no savings, so I'd have to fast
from food and shelter; peeling off my shell
would make my daily life a numbing hell.

I am reserved, withdrawn; when I emote
it is the actor's mask that magnifies
my volume and that shapes what I, by rote,
have learned to say. Even when I surprise
my audience with glimpses of my dreams,
I hide my inner self with all that seems.

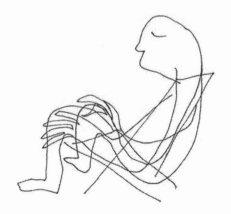

PET SCANS

OCCASIONAL CAT

Mister Buster was not my cat, but he
would live at my house whenever Daisy
would win some sort of poetic award—
a prize, a grant; a down payment toward
a house came when she won a fellowship—
and then she would spend a month in Europe
with her partner and then her husband, Jim.
She'd pack up Mister Buster and bring him

over to my place. This was when I lived
in a rented rowhouse: two floors above
a basement through which Mr. Buster could
roam and rest and slip unnoticed and hide;
and evenings, when I'd settle down and read,
he'd lie against my upper back and sleep.

1. THE EDUCATED GRASSHOPPER

They say that if you put a grasshopper
in a jar, he will learn that he can jump
only as far as the invisible
but impenetrable surface will al-
low. Even if you let him out in the
wide world after a while, his leaps will al-
ways be limited intrinsically
by what he learned in that little envi-
ronment, where his horizons were brought for-
cibly against his most delicate man-
dibles and his forehead was battered by
something he couldn't predict would be there,
and even the broad sky was distorted
by the vector of a translucent curve.

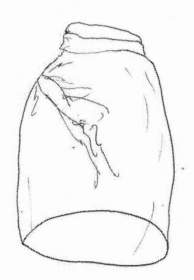

2. FALL

The grasshopper everybody admires —
that Romantic, sky-leaper, denizen
of summer, surrounded by supple stalks
of froth-topped grasses that dance with the wind.
Is it the grasshopper who fiddles, or
is it his cousin the cicada? No
matter: we're not entomologizing
here, we're ruminating about fables:

the grasses, much more lithe than the rigid
oak, still fall to the scythe, the cicada's
cadences fall with the flamboyant leaves,
and the grasshopper's balletic legs seize
up, grinding at the joints, his carapace
a hollow husk. The ant wins in the end.

3. SPARROW

The ant wins in the end. The sparrow, drunk
on pyracantha berries, smacks against
the living room's plate-glass window, neck snapped,
thuds on the lawn. An hour later, ants
form a two-way assembly line, bucket
brigade lugging the blood and whatever
other furniture they can dismantle
from the body the sparrow's abandoned.

This was no skylark, connecting this earth
with the realm of the Luminosities,
occasional Bridge that made daring raids
on the Infinite. This was a bundle
of feathers and twigs for gleaners to pick
apart as grammarians grade papers.

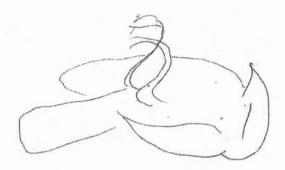

4. SUBWAY

As grammarians grade papers, so ants
file through the bodies of the world, the black
lines flexing in the sunlight, blood pulsing
without the vessels to contain them. They

contain themselves, the ants crawling over
each other so as not to fractal off
and subdivide the stream with the threat of
chaos. The ants are orderly, like a

muscle fiber, like commuters on the
subway, like a python that engorges
a jungle boar and widens all along

itself, accommodates that bulk as it
is stripped of tough hide, muscle, tendon, fat,
and clean bones are delivered at the end.

5. ANT, ALONE

From one of those glistening files of ants
that connects a sudden source of food—road
kill, fish flopped out of water, seagull dropped
from the sky—you will occasionally

notice a single ant that has struck out
into a divagation from the flow
of the collective. In a wavering
loop, the ant will stagger beneath its crumb,

bump against pebbles and glebes, its spindles
pick out the pathways the water has gouged,
all the while its antennae frantically

trying to figure out how to get back
into the comforting compaction crowds
exchange for the nakedness of freedom.

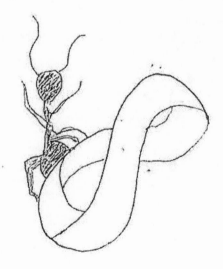

FOURTH HOUSE THUMBNAIL

That tiny bedroom, maybe ten by twelve,
is not just where I slept, but where my desk
and chair under the built-in bookcase sat.
I had a dictionary and a lamp—
harsh fluorescent white—a can of pencils,
pens, and a compass on my right, the window
also on my right but behind my back.
There I'd perch on weekday nights for six years,
when I would stay at school and walk home late
just in time for dinner, then climb upstairs
while the rest of the family watched TV.
Three closed doors kept most of the laughter out
of my ears. My consciousness was an ant
that slowly would meander across the page.

CROW

I imagine Ted Hughes pulling over
to the shoulder before dawn
between the road and the river.
Frozen grass shatters, dark tracks parallel
      in the gleaming rime.
He kills the motor,
listens to the unconscious water wrestle.

     The bathwater, invisible,
grows tepid. Wind heaves, blind, against
the slant of the skylight.
Cars start, dogs bark.
            I rose early today,
twisted amid sheets. Ted Hughes is several
years dead, long after Sylvia. Wolves howl
from his *Selected Poems*, stark black
print planted, scattered abstractions of sound
silenced over the snowy paper.

THE FLIES OF MID-AUTUMN

The flies of mid-autumn are fat and slow.
Their buzzing is over an octave too low.
They are the survivors: there is no limit
to how large they can grow, but as long as they eat, they expand.

They are anachronistic, like the last
Civil War veterans in the mid-twentieth century
or like the few most ancient of the vultures
that might have feasted, fledglings, on horses
slaughtered at Gettysburg.

The flies of mid-autumn seem undecided as to
what they should do or where they should go,
as opposed to the flies of summer, whose apparent
diffidence and divagation are deliberate manoeuvres,
inscribed in their genes, to wear down our wariness.
There is one in my bathroom right now, in
early November, as big as a toad,
voice deep as a bumblebee's, a prune with wings.

FIRST FACELESS

FISHING STORY

They say the Soul chooses its own parents before birth.
   – New Age truism

What did I have in mind before I had a brain?
Floating invisible and incorporeal above a flesh
couple making awkward love? Awkward, because
no one could see them but each other, and their own
eyes were closed, and it was unpracticed, unrehearsed,
each performance was the real thing, on an unlit
stage, audience of each other, giving themselves up
to something genetic, scripts unread, words from

the movies giving way to gasps, groans, inarticulate
cries of surprise, unknowing whether from pain
or something bordering on a mysticism neither believed
in, clenching, knocking, drilling, perhaps a bite
the bait for which was the possibility of me,
sucked into the zygote with unaccustomed gravity.

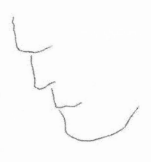

53

BACKGROUND

We didn't touch each other very much
in my family when I was growing
into myself, into that person which
I was going to be. As for sowing
what you will later reap, the lack of touch
planted the seeds of a way of knowing
which in some ways is especially rich—
that of the individual rowing

alone in his boat just beyond the reeds
in the still water with indefinite
depth. So the isolated reader reads,
disconnected from the immediate
environment, while the oars' delicate
dip in the dark pond suggests what he needs.

AGRICULTURAL RESEARCH STATION, BELTSVILLE, MD

There was a cow with a window in it
where my father worked when I was a kid.
Dad didn't work with any cows, much less
the one with a window in it: his job
was in personnel. He dealt with human
inconsistencies and deficiencies
and hirings and firings, and at the end
of his career he negotiated

between employee's unions on one side
and the Department of Agriculture
as the employer. I never did see
that cow's window real close—it was more like
a porthole in a Laundromat machine
where the spin cycle moved really slow.

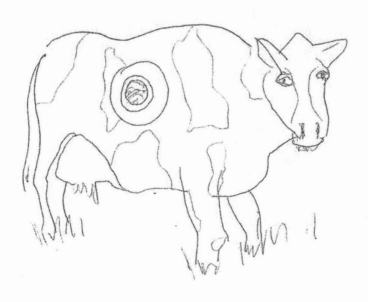

CAN'T THINK

Why is it I can't think of a moment
like that potato peeling of Heaney's
sonnet where he, alone with his mother,
share, wordless, that cold kniving together?

When I write "can't think" I see Thanksgiving
nearly twenty years ago when I asked
Dad on a walk and Mom in the living
room, seated behind her *Washington Post*
in that corner occupied by her wing
chair if they believed in life after death?

Dad said "Nope. When I die I'll be as dead
as a dog." Mom, startled from her reading,
her eyes as lively as I'd ever seen,
said no, but she couldn't imagine not thinking.

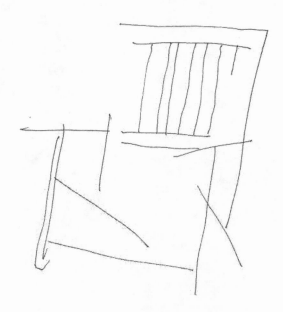

HUGS

Where did I first learn to withdraw
into myself whenever someone hugged me
and later, whenever I hugged someone else,
silently saying, *Here I am,*
spread like a flying squirrel all over you
and you the air the I float over, but also
the earth I'm afraid of smacking against,
breaking my jaw; my fingers will snap

when I bellyflop against your slapping
waters, my ribs will shatter, dinosaur
skeleton tottering in the quake museum,
my sternum pop open, a sardine tin,
and my heart, sprung from its cage, will panic,
a hamster *spastic in slippery innards?*

MORNING MIRROR

Like a knee, my father's forehead
emerges from my face as my hair
recedes, dune grass thinned in face
of the sea and its constant wind.

Like a dune, skin emerges as the sea
washes in and then recedes, this tide
pool, still, left behind. I gaze daily
into it to discern, scry, the future,

but I have it backwards; it is the past
that attracts my notice and I see my
self fall into my father's habits
that cast shadows under my eyes
and the dune grasses thinned by the sea's
wind cede place to a knobby knee.

NAKEDNESS

There is the newborn's nakedness when first
stripped of the mother, then the nakedness
of schoolchildren showering after gym,
then the nakedness of pubescence,
alone in the family bathroom, strange
sensitivities and delicate hairs
in formerly pristine places.
                                    There is
the nakedness of newlyweds, the catch
in the throat, the conjunction of pleasure
and torture, increasingly easier
if less intense pleasure, then nakedness
of anonymous professionals.

Then there's the nakedness of camp inmates
queuing for showers in the early 'forties.

BILATERAL ASYMMETRY

BILATERAL ASYMMETRY

My right side, my adroit side, is tighter;
my sinister side is much more relaxed.
My dominant side is more insecure
since it always has to be capable;
my submissive side's used to giving in:
sloppiness is expected. The right takes
over, the head pulled close to the shoulder
as if I'm always listening closer

to what the left brain commands, pulling strings
on the opposite side of the body.
The left side, where the heart lives, the right brain
loosely directs, taking a wait-and-see
attitude. Most of the body's water,
it reflects; let it shift along ley lines.

FEAR AND SYMMETRY

Symmetry is natural. At birth you
could be photographed, the photo halved,
and one half folded over, doubled,
and no one be the wiser. At the first
broken arm, when you fall from the slide
during recess in first or second grade,
you learn to favor the limb with the wound,
which the other side adapts to, a kind,
stronger sibling letting the weaker one
rest so it can heal.
                      But after a while
the body thickens on the stronger side,
which develops a proud solicitude.
This is reflected in the expression
of the face, half-serious, half-fool.

PRESCRIPTION

That professor at Tufts who interviewed
a half dozen of us some forty-two
years ago singled me out to suggest
I read *The Ginger Man* by Donleavy.
I didn't, though I have remembered it
for these four decades and purchased a used
paperback of it a few years ago,
and have even read the first chapter.

I can see him now: close-trimmed greying beard,
herringbone jacket with elbow patches,
suggesting this novel as antidote,
as I see it now, for the earnestness
I presented then, suppressing my id
like an obedient dog. *Loosen up, kid!*

THE ELEMENTS

Boy Scouts was where we forced ourselves outside
for whole afternoons hiking down the creek
or for whole weekends camping out in snow
shivering in our sleeping bags at dawn.
The rest of our lives were spent indoors;
                                        just
walking to the bus and an hour for gym
and walking through the parking lot at school
to bypass the long convoluted hall
to the band room in the far wing exposed
us to the elements—wind, rain, and sun—

that indoors we read about at best—*and*
the yonge sonne hath in the Ram his
halfe course y-ronne—not knowing why
like the small fools nature pricked our hearts so.

TICKLE TORTURE

It would be hilarious if it were
not so deadly, the old classical mode
of death by helpless laughter, once achieved
by binding someone to a chair, the legs

horizontal, tied in place to keep them
from shifting and from loosening the ropes
and from moving the feet, having been dipped
in salt water, from where the goats lick them

on the soles, the salt tastes so good they don't
want this source to slip away from their rough
tongues, although the feet, stimulated by the

tongues' abrasive surfaces, jerk the legs;
with helpless diaphragm's ragged spasms
the man barks, dying ridiculously.

CÉRÉMONIE

CONFESSION

She asked me if I wrote confessional
poetry and I had to admit I
did, as everything I write down has to
do with whatever is on my mind when
I'm writing it: my sleep patterns, any
dreams I may have remembered or if I
remember a fragment a single shot
I write that down and follow the pathway

that opens up before me, tracing where
I may have gone even if I didn't
actually go there when I was dead
to the world and I was taking the deep
road into the Lower World unfolding
before me holding my pen before me.

SOMETIMES I JUST SIT

Sometimes I just sit and stare at nothing.
Biff Mitthoefer, in that yin yoga class,
said to me, "You sure do know how to *sit,*"
meaning *meditate*, is how I took it.
But often, I just sit, don't meditate,
or levitate in any way. I sit.

Perhaps that is the way that I will be
in general when I am very old.
I will stand, or walk around the house, stare
at objects that don't represent ideas,
but just are: brute, insensible matter,
which is, after all, our matrix, *mater*.

My womb will be my apartment, cluttered
or bare, with unopened books everywhere.

OSSIPOEISIS

Poems should be dictated through the bones,
as muscles stretch and relax with the wind.
The nerves threaded through the muscles have sinned,
communicating *pleasure* to the brains

all dressed in black, Bunraku puppeteers
clustering around their marionette.
The puppeteers, as pushy as you get,
dominate the body, solicitors

telling it to lift this finger, drop that
relationship since it doesn't bring much
of value in beyond a seldom touch—
an old bachelor ankled by a cat.

That's why poems should be channeled through the bones:
no verse of much value comes from the brains.

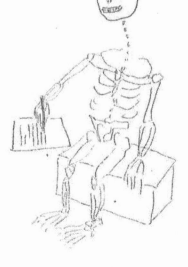

PRIVATE INTRICACIES

At the age of six, I was pigeon-toed,
then was diagnosed with falling arches,
as if there were aqueducts and churches
crumbling while a stream of invaders flowed

across the isolated island of
my body. I learned to pull my laces
tight on my feet. Is it on this basis
that I learned to count syllables and love

cleverly threaded-in slanting end rhymes
like unexpected passes or end runs
that suddenly solve the congested knot

of rushers and blockers in pickup games
in my neighbors' front yard? No crowds in stands,
just a kid who's pulled all his laces taut.

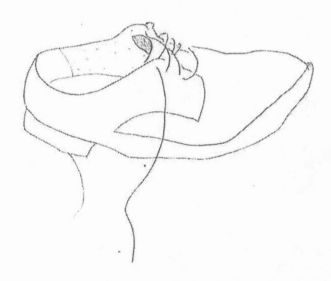

THE ELVES KNOW

The elves know they are the elite, they know
their long intricate poems by heart, recite
them as they contemplate the sunset leaves.

The elves have interminable evenings
after they've returned from work, are content
with having totally dispatched duties
during the day. Nobody can question
whether they've lifted their share of the load.

Therefore, their evenings are sacrosanct. They
dine with an exquisite presence, signal
each other subtly across the table.

Then, their Noh drama, unchanged since the ninth
century, unfolds before their eyes. String
quartets on their stereos afterwards.

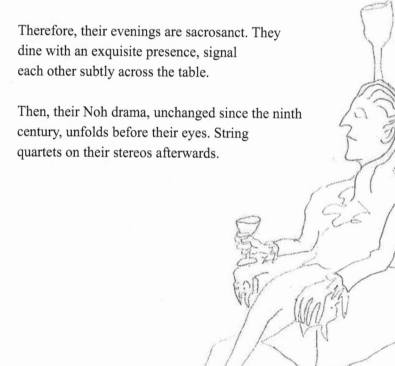

CÉRÉMONIE

When I first light an incense stick, the flame
replaces the dark tip with a liquid
flower I allow to grow, though slowly,
so the stick will heat with a dull gold glow.

I hold the stick straight, ceremonial
sword, hieratic torch, Neolithic
illumination for shamans to show
incised bison on the crevice wall

to the Called young in initiation.
In the medicine cabinet mirror
the flame throws shadows over my aged face.

Softly, I blow the flame into a spathe
that leans back lazily from the incense
pistil, ecstatic in its little death.

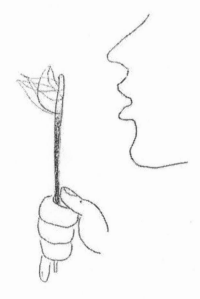

ARS BREVIS VITRINA OBSCURA

LYING AT THE BASE

When I don't have any particular
topic to write about, I will sometimes
write ten syllables per line for fourteen
lines to fulfill my self-imposed project
of writing a sonnet every day. Sure,
it is in that case a blank sonnet, not
even in iambic pentameter,
but I do this to keep up my writing

practice in the expectation that one
day something lying at the base of my
limbic node will awaken, an ancient

dragon, perhaps, that will peer through the dark
cavern of my cranium, clear its throat,
then light my brain with a primal fire.

PRIMING THE PUMP

As if I needed inspiration, prompt
for writing, I automatically reach
for the anthology—one of several—
to read in, get the rhythm started, set
my mind in a certain direction, mode
of dealing with my current quandary.
Instead of a sonnet, I remember
Berryman's *Dream Song*, forget the number,

I stared at Ruin. Ruin stared right back.
Perfect iambic pentameter line!
Berryman always wrote with a certain
class, but his life was a mess. All the same,
he had friends who'd loan him a hundred bucks,
and once he received the Pulitzer Prize.

INFLUENCZA

Often, when I sit to write a sonnet,
I'll read something first to put it in gear;
and what I read will inflect what I write.
Sometimes it's thematic, like erotic
verse will inform my vocabulary
with body parts and those hidden juices
that charge us with subtle awarenesses.
Sometimes it's formal, like I'll try rhyming

or string out sung sounds along a taut line.
At other times, I will try for prosy,
commonplace diction without evident
attention paid to rhythmic qualities,
in an attempt to shock the reader who
expects to be transported into trance.

TranceLate

ALIGNMENT

Thomas Wyatt's original sonnets,
not strictly iambic pentameter,
are syllabic and allow natural
variations in the vernacular
idioms of the tongue to give muscle
to the line, as rivers flex and gurgle
over stones on the uneven bottom.

When you split logs, as evenly as they
may be sawn into segments, set the maul's
edge in approximate alignment with
the lightning-shaped capillaries of faults,
such as a perceptive friend will sense in
even the most harmonious couple,
then crack the log and feed it to the fire.

INVISIBLE HAND

Sometimes I pretend that some other hand
reaches into my own and uses it
like a glove, perhaps to throw off some
karmic police, leaving my fingerprints
on the pen, having left words not my own,
an alien creature's pawprints in the snow,
or even a drawing the stylistic
traits of which diverge from my own manner.

I *pretend*; sometimes I so much as wish
that what we back in the 'seventies called
The Higher Self would squeeze through the chakra
at the fontanelle and fill my wet flesh
with its fiery lines to my fingertips
and leave me a message for when I wake.

READING WRITING RILKE

I can read Rilke in translation, but
I still don't understand. O Orphic voice,
that only flows in German when read out
loud! I don't understand it either. Choice
between images that the inner eye
sees materialize in the temple,
to direct sun shining there from the sky,
only memories of things, so simple,

a pedigree that goes back to childhood:
sun, wind, clouds, grass, the coffee grounds of earth!
And when I read the original,
my voice rings as if it were understood,
though not by *my* mind. The music gives birth
to a grove in which I am marginal.

UBER BLUMEN UND MADCHEN
nostalgia for a lost mistranslation

I can always translate from a text, but
how can I translate something from the past?
I started out with a Rilke sonnet
about flowers cut by young girls, addressed

to the flowers, but really for the girls
who cut them. I envision daffodils—
I can't say why; it was not in the words
of the poems—perhaps it was the frills

of their skirts, wrinkle-enfolded petals
of the yellow flowers atop the stalks
planted like not-quite flexible green stakes,

scissored from the ground, then placed in vases
where they stand, tilted, as if at their ease,
proffering flounces of summery dresses.

AFTER RILKE

Young girls' smooth pale hands arranging flowers,
cut for the occasion in the garden,
in cut-crystal vases, cool skin, long thin
sensitive fingers tilting daffodils
against each other, their tall stalks leaning
lightly, hollow, stiff and stiffening with
the sudden seepage of water upwards
through osmosis of xylem and phloem,

hands, wrists, forearms, radius and ulna
rotate slightly, just sufficiently to shift
the nearly weightless stilts of brilliant jonquils,
like the sleek, slender, gently tapering
legs of young women starting to blossom,
scalloped skirts gliding against the light thighs.

ENJAMBMENT

Life goes on, but individual poems
stop. The most you can hope for is the line
that doesn't end with a period. You
are suspended in the middle of a

sentence, possibly look up, then resume
reading as if the music never stopped,
as if everyone didn't have to dive
for the chairs, of which there were always one

too few. This was before birthdays returned
with such increasing rapidity that
you lost count, the world hurtling around the
small yellow star, the entire universe

flashing past your bewildered eyes until,
like a premeditated sonnet, all is still.

INVERSION OF, NO QUESTION

For older poets Latin having learned
when rather in the sun they'd have been playing,
when rhymes were seeking they, never spurned
reversed of words the order from their saying.

Aback when taken by a thought though random,
as if composing in a tongue inflected
multiplicity without ends in tandem
together pieced be meaning can detected.

As in the mirror sees the subject th'object
perception of precise, himself reversed,
so on the page pursues with pen his project
last arrived at what conceived he first.

Whatever touches convoluted thought,
sense slips back on self, Baroque with, fraught.

SILENT ECHO

PAIRING

The drive for rhyme must have some subtle root
in our drive for pairing, with right and left,
with up and down, with clumsy and adept;
in walking, alternating foot with foot.
The same with sex: a woman's not a man
minus a penis, carrying a womb,
with mandarin-useless long hair and comb,
and certainly not who invented sin.

The pairing is of similars but not
identicals, like pairing sea with bird
or, through the lungs' root network, blood with breath:
it is the slant rhyme that pairs death with birth,
lining them up like cutting-board with bread,
tying them for a time with a neat slipknot.

CONVENTION

How many poems basically say I
desire that woman, I wish she'd desire
me, or, assuming she already does,
would show it to me more incontrovertibly?

That coy one, who occasionally flits
across the edge of my peripheral
actual sight and haunts my virtual
vision, has the *virtù* of spring flowers

and I could lie and dream of her for hours,
elbows on ground, jaws on hands, where thought sits
and sketches in my mind indelibly

the graceful neck of that tenderest doe
who has lit in my dark heartwood a fire
and then run gracefully, swiftly off, shy.

MOON'S ODE TO EARTH

I want to fall into you. Your
hot core, though hidden, draws me
as a caricature of a lover
always closing for the embrace

as you in your curvature veer
ever away; you show me your
cold shoulder. The gravity
of this situation is only

balanced by my constancy
of impetus. It is you
versus inertia; I average
both attractions into a near perfect

circle. Rumors of our fusion
are a quirk of Romantic illusion.

LONG/DISTANCE

Longing creates distance, I said when she
asked how I was doing. *Longing creates
distance,* she said to herself as she wiped
the window clear, frowning slightly. *No*
I interrupted, *distance is created by
longing* as I frowned to myself and *no,
distance <u>creates</u> longing. No,* she said
upon reflection or perhaps clarity, *longing*

*creates distance because when you long for
something you put distance between you.
So I was right in the first place,* I
said, not quite convinced. *I don't think
I've learned that lesson yet,* one of us said.
We'll continue this later, she said, leaving.

HORTUS CONCLUSUS

A man and a woman in their late twenties
bend their heads together, towards each other,
in this candid color picture.
What does she hold, tiny, between them
that holds their focused attention?
They are oblivious to the magnificent
walled Moorish medieval garden
of the Alcázar rising around them.

"Paradise" was a Persian word
for "enclosed garden surrounding a fountain"
hidden in the midst of a vast desert.
Paradise, I now know, is the past
where they peer and smile at a shared secret
with, floating unknown above them, a rose glowing.

SUPERHERO WEAKNESS

If I were Green Lantern and you Wonder
Woman, we'd fly helices around each
other as in a whirl of DNA.
I'd admire your tiara and ask you
about your sunken home of Atlantis,
and you'd remark how my green face mask made
me more mysterious. I'd create an
emerald palace for you with my ring,
where I'd gaze into your unobstructed
sky-blue eyes, and when you'd rise and stalk off
on your long, elegantly muscled legs
to pour from a viridian decanter,
you'd capture me with your golden lasso
against which my power ring would be helpless.

HERSELF

Enchantment with the sound of wordless song
or with songs in tongues I don't understand
or even with low wind chimes in a breeze
would so suspend me from the task at hand
that I would find myself afloat, my gaze
unfocused on the Boston Ivy, dense
as a waterfall of various greens
reflecting flecks of light amid shadows.

This was the realm of the Lady, whom trees
sheltered from summer's unrelenting sun;
I never saw her clearly, she was all
women I'd ever desired in one
whose face constantly shifted as the leaves
shifted, half-erasing as they revealed.

le Gentil Gérard

GRIND OF BEING

PRIZE

A child brings home a sheet crayoned with ships
or teepees lined up alongside a sun
outlined in bold black and with scarlet lips
and generic animals on the run
for no reason at all except sheer joy
to be in the universe in the mind
of a kindergarten or first-grade boy
or girl where the weather is always kind.

Then again there are terrors of the dark
under the bed, where who knows what could reach
out and grab the ankles when the child must
go to the potty down the hall. They teach
you to suppress these for a life of work
and you lose the spark of what you loved most.

BOULOT

When someone does something for a living
that doesn't nourish his spirit, he drinks
endless glasses of hard liquor evenings,
like my friend who works in finance, who thinks
he's sold out, who really wanted to teach
but then bought his house and couldn't afford
the mortgage—a teacher's pay wouldn't stretch
that far. Last night I saw the barmaid pour

him a fresh scotch each time his drink's level
sank, without having to be reminded,
and walked home, knowing I would have to teach
next week for the first time this new term, reach
out to reluctant students blindsided
by requirements, who think I'm the devil.

RECONFIGURATION

They say that if I stay positive
in my attitude towards unfolding
situations at this time in my life,
that positive vibe will reverberate

and result in more positive outcomes.
I faithfully buy lottery tickets,
one at a time—no use dissipating
the energy with a dozen—and smile

at the woman in the Plexiglas booth,
who smiles back—she knows what I want by now
and has it waiting for me when I come—

and wishes me good luck. As for the rest,
I try to reconfigure what seem to
be setbacks as steps to transformation.

SUPERFLUITY

When you've said what you need to say, but still
have to put pen to paper and drag it
across—like a plow turning up rich soil
or like a metal detector, magnet
at the end of a handled staff, dowsing
for treasures hidden underneath the sand,
you don't expect to find something rousing
to say, but hope something will come to hand

that you can unfold like an open mind,
tickled as if by your pen become wind,
a gentle wind, at first, that caresses,
then gathers power and speed till it whirls
around everything that's been your life, hurls
your books and furniture into abysses.

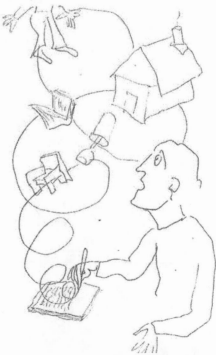

REAL MAGIC

Real magic involves metamorphosis
of one thing into a wholly other,
as of that wise nearly 500-year
-old phoenix those children found in a book
I discovered in my school library
and have just remembered now, 50 years
later. At his instructions, the children
helped him settle on his pyre, then lit it,

weeping as they saw their friend turn to ash,
then staring amazed as the phoenix emerged
younger, stronger, unwrinkled, glorious
stretching his wings for the very first time,
glancing at them without recognition,
launched into his new life, never to return.

TIME FILES

NOW WE TURN TWO

I am going in today, Saturday,
to grade exams, and work out in the gym,
then to my office-mate's sixtieth
birthday party. He's younger than I am
by some months,though sixty is not the real
pivotal point of this portion of life:
it is fifty-nine, approximately,
depending on stations and apparent

retrograde motion of planet Saturn,
for now we turn two from a saturnine
standpoint; we have lived our youth, then matured,
spending decades being responsible,
and now it is time to become wizards
or slowly dilapidate like King Lear.

SOUNDINGS

The knocks and skitters and shiftings of weight
play this apartment like the hollow drum
it is. I hear the woman upstairs, cat
a rapid series of taps to her firm
tread, and then I hear the flowing through the throat
the hiss of water. She is at the sink
doing one of the several things that
one does there: wash, pouring oneself a drink.

Whatever it was, she has stopped doing
it, and I feel occasional groaning
boards as she crosses her floor, my ceiling.
The guy one floor down must listen to me,
though I tread lightly as someone stealing
every thing I treasure, silent as time.

THE LAST TIME WE DANCED TO THE BEATLES

I threw my knee out—not the one I broke
in the bike accident in France, the one
on the other leg, which was jealous
of my favoring the broken leg for so long,
so started acting up to call attention
to itself. It was all early Beatles
the DJ was playing, so vigorous
with the drumline thumping its steady way

underneath the two- and three-part vocals
about holding your hand, or wanting to,
and offering for you to drive my car
under the shining stars and the dark sky
while I just wanted to slow dance with you
as they were softly playing *Yesterday.*

REALITY CHECK

in memoriam Francess Lantz 1952-2004

When I contacted Fran, or the other
way around, we exchanged thumbnail sketches
of how our lives had gone since we had last
as college classmates been together.
I'd gone to her wedding some years ago;
she'd gotten divorced, then remarried twice,
written and published over a score of books,
had kids, then cancer, had her womb removed.

I'd been married once, for eighteen years,
was still reciting litanies of pain
which I did to Fran, said it all again
until she said, on email, look—here's
the difference: I've done divorce three times,
you once. Also, I have almost died.

WHEN I DIE I HOPE THEY WILL PLAY MOZART

When I die I hope they will play Mozart—
the clarinet concerto and quintet—
at the funeral or memorial
service, whichever they decide to hold.

In either case, I will be a phantom
without bones under the myrtles, not that
I know what myrtles look like, but I see
a purplish shade in the mind's grove Monet

painted for me or was that Wolf Kahn? I
will be detached from all the cathartic
tears, larynxes played roughly as Malcolm
Goldstein's threnody for one string, for I

will hear that last movement of the Mozart,
written two months before his own death, sparkle.

WINTER YIN

A single bird on a naked tree, black,
both, silhouetted by the pre-dawn light.
Still winter, so the leaves, long
gone, leave slender branches, like the fine
bones of a completely eaten fish. This
black skeleton, as opposed to the white
stiff feathery filaments of that dead
feast cleaned as if by a punctilious
cat, absorbs all colors, so reflects back
none, but has sucked them in to the very
pith and has stored them there in its sluggish
sap, of which the virtue, released next spring,
engendered, will floor me with a long string
of buds, blossoms, and this huddled bird's song.

Don Riggs has been writing and drawing since the 6th grade. Over the years he has gone through a number of stylistic evolutions. In three previously published chapbooks (as in *Bilateral Asymmetry*) he integrates drawing and words.

All of the drawings in this book were done by Don Riggs, but several were copied from or in the style of: George Perez, Neal Adams, Saul Steinberg, Michelangelo Buonarroti, Jean-Honoré Fragonard, Robert M. Place, the Waite-Rider Tarot deck, Antoine de Saint-Exupéry, Boris Vallejo, M.C. Escher, Leonard Baskin, and anonymous engravers in 17th-century alchemical texts.

Made in the USA
Lexington, KY
09 May 2014